Effect of Alkali Silica Reaction and Change of Temperature on Strength Of Self -Compacting- Concrete (SCC) Assessed Friction Transferring Method

Vol. 1

Esmaeil Yahya Zadeh Moghaddam

Title: Effect of Alkali Silica Reaction and Change of Temperature on Strength of Self-Compacting-Concrete (SCC) Assessed Friction Transferring Method (Vol. 1)

Author: Esmaeil Yahya Zadeh Moghaddam

Translator: Azam Nikbakht

Cover Design: Somaye Babaei Tarkami

Publisher: American Academic Research, USA

ISBN: 978-1-947464-20-9

2020 © Esmaeil Yahya Zadeh Moghaddam

All Rights Reserved for The Author

Contents

Chapter One

Introduction and History 5

1-1 Introduction 6

   1-1-1 Introduction 6

   1-1-2 Research Method: 7

1-2 History 7

   1-2-1 11-year analysis of self-compacting concrete samples 9

   1-2-1-1 New features 10

   1-2-1-2 Compressive strength 10

   1-2-1-3 Compounds and components 11

   1-2-1-4 mixing ratio 12

   1-2-1-5 Amounts of materials 12

   1-2-1-6 Properties of the mixture 13

   1-2-2 Execution examples of self-compacting concrete [7] 13

   1- Akashi-Kaiko suspension bridge 13

   2- The walls of the huge LNG tanks of Japan Osaka Gas Company[7] 14

   3- Midsummer Place, located in London, England. [8] 15

   4- Immersed tunnel project in Kobe, Japan. [8] 16

   5- Landmark Tower in Yokohama, Japan. [9] 17

Chapter Two

Definitions and review of research 20

2-1 Definitions 21

   2-1-1 Mineral additives 21

   2-1-2 Chemical additives 21

   2-1-3 Adhesive 21

   2-1-4 Filling capability (unlimited flow capability) 21

   2-1-5 Mortar 21

   2-1-6 Cement paste 21

   2-1-7 Passability (limited flow capability) 21

   2-1-8 Powder (fine material) 21

   2-1-9 Self-compacting concrete 22

2-1-10 Resistance to separation (stability) 22
2-1-11 Efficiency 22
2-1-12 Chemical additives 22
2-1-13 Mineral additives 22
2-1-13-1 Types of mineral additives 22
2-1-14 Powder for melting iron 23
2-1-15 Glass filler powder 23
2-1-16 Pigment 23
2-1-17 Fibers 23

2.2 Fresh self-compacting concrete tests 23
2-2-1 Slump flow test and slump flow time up to 50 cm 24
2-2-1-1 Experimental steps 25
2-2-1-2 Interpretation of results 25
2-2-2 J-shaped ring test 27
2.2.3 Test the V-shaped funnel and increase the time of the V-shaped funnel in five minutes ...28
2-2-3-1 Experimental steps 29
2-2-3-2 Interpretation of test results 29
2-2-4 L-shaped mold test 29
2-2-4-1 Experimentation steps 30
2-2-4-2 Interpretation of results 30
2-2-5 U-shaped mold test 32
2-2-6 Fill box test 1 34
2-2-7 Sieve Stability Test 35
2-2-8 Orimet method 35
2-2-8-1 Interpretation of results 37
2-2-9 Session column method 37

2-3 tests performed 38
2-3-1 Test to determine the resistance of concrete to ice cycle and ice melting 38
2-3-2 Alkaline silica reaction test 39

2-4 Rheology self-compacting concrete 39
2-4-1 Performance of self-compacting concrete 39
2-4-2 Filling capability 40
2-4-3 Separation resistance 40

2-4-4 Crossing ability 40

Chapter Three

A variety of methods for determining the strength of concrete in situ 42

3- Types of methods for determining the strength of concrete in situ 43

3-1 Non-destructive tests...43
3-1-1 Ultrasonic wave velocity test 43
3-1-1-2 Scope of application: 44
3-1-2 Eschmidt hammer..44
3-1-2-1 Scope of application: 47
3-1-3 The method of penetrating waves in the ground (Crevasse Wave) 47
3-1-4 Reinforced concrete cutting method (Tomography)..50
3-1-4-1 Scope of application:...50

3-2 Semi-destructive experiments..50
3-2-1 Intrusion resistance test 50
3-2-2-Extraction test (Pullout)..51
3-2-2-1 Important points in the extraction method 52
3-2-3 Twist Off method 52
3-2-3-1 Scope of application 54
3-2-4 friction transferring method 54
3-2-4-1 Scope of application 57

Chapter One

Introduction and History

1-1 Introduction

1-1-1 Introduction

In concrete structures, to achieve the required strength and reduce porosity and air inside the concrete and achieve the reliability of concrete is vibrated in different ways. With the increasing development of concrete work and the relative shortage of skilled workers or their negligence in the workshops when pouring concrete in the formwork, especially in places where there is rebar density, the vibration operation is not done completely and correctly and finally the desired mechanical properties of concrete Does not turn. Therefore, making a concrete without the need for vibration has always been researched by scientists in this field who can add a substance to concrete to achieve the important that the construction of self-compacting concrete (SCC) is the result of this research.

As a result, self-compacting concrete is concrete that flows under the weight under the mold and completely fills the mold. In fact, it is concrete that does not need to be vibrated to be in the desired location or compaction, even if the reinforcement is dense. [1]

Self-compacting concrete has properties such as greater stability against detachment and wetting and has a higher ductility that is widely used in construction. These properties are achieved despite a mixing scheme and the use of advanced additives and more accurate selection of aggregates. These additives in combination with more dough, due to having no negative effect on increasing thermal cracks with

The use of replacing part of the cement with various fillers can be extracted[2]

In structures that have limited space and structural members with dense reinforcement, this concrete is used for the correct and accurate execution of the desired structure.

Among the advantages of self-compacting concrete, which can be mentioned in the types of prestressed, prefabricated and in-situ concrete, are the following:

1- Eliminate vibration noise at the place of using this type of concrete in the factory or workshop.
2- Do not use a vibrator as a result of removing defects that may occur due to vibration.
3- Using fewer workers.
4- Increasing the construction speed.
5- Improving the quality and durability of concrete.
6- Higher resistance. [3]

From the economic point of view of self-compacting concrete, due to the mixing design and components of the mixture, as well as the use of superplasticizers and additives, this concrete has become more expensive. However, due to the elimination of vibration, we see a reduction in the number of workers and construction time of the structure, both of which compensate for the increase in cost, and in bulk concreting, the use of self-compacting concrete is quite economical and cost-effective.

The disadvantages of this concrete are when the psyche of the concrete is used by using lubricating or super-lubricating additives in the concrete too much, which causes separation in the concrete and damages the quality of the concrete.

1-1-2 Research Method:

The idea was first proposed by Okamura[4] in Japan and eventually spread to Europe and other parts of the world. While today, all over the world, research is being done on such concrete.

In Iran, the use of self-compacting concrete began several years ago and its benefits have been used. The mixing components and the ratio of compounds in this concrete are very sensitive and it loses its compaction capability with a slight change, so this suitable mixing design is very sensitive due to the available materials.

In Iran, due to the abundance of natural resources for the production of cement and concrete, the use of concrete structures in various projects has developed a lot. Unfortunately, the lack of technical workers or their absence in most parts of the country causes a great decline in concrete quality and waste of national capital and irreparable human damage in natural disasters, and in the study of these structures, insufficient concrete density is clearly observed. Therefore, using self-compacting concrete instead of ordinary concrete to solve this problem seems logical.

It should be noted that in this book, the mixing design that has been previously researched has been used [30], which I mention has been worked on several mixing designs and according to the best case (in terms of resistance) in this research That mixing scheme has been used. The three mixing designs accepted in the study are by replacing 25, 35 and 45% of cement with fly ash, and in all three designs the amount of superplasticizer and to some extent the water to powder ratio are affected by the change in the amount of filler. The effect of alkaline silica reaction on the strength of concrete according to ASTM 1260 standard on three samples of self-compacting concrete and one sample of ordinary vibrating concrete (NC) as a control sample.

The second test of the effect of temperature changes on the strength of self-compacting concrete according to C666-84 standard was performed on a sample of self-compacting concrete and a sample of ordinary vibrating concrete.

1-2 History

Evolution of self-compacting concrete is one of the most valuable human successes in the manufacturing industry to overcome the problems of ordinary concrete. Self-compacting concrete can be used for pumping at longer distances due to its high psychological properties and resistance to particle decomposition under the influence of factors such as workers' skills or mixing design. [4]

The concept of self-compacting concrete was first proposed by Professor Okamura 1 in 1986, but a prototype was developed in 1988 by Professor Ozawa II, a professor at the University of Tokyo in Japan.

Self-compacting concrete at that time in order to improve the durability and strength of concrete structures produced since then, several researches were conducted in this field and this type of concrete was practically used by large construction companies in the construction industry. [4]

The research was conducted to design compaction testing methods from the perspective of converting self-compacting concrete into a standard concrete. Since self-compacting concrete is very compact, no additional internal and external vibration is required to compress it. This type of concrete flows like honey and after concreting, it has a very smooth and soft surface. [4]

In general, self-compacting concrete is not a new product. Specific applications of concrete, such as underwater concreting, have always required a combination so that it can be used without compacting the concrete.

In the structure of primary self-compacting concretes, the main material was cement paste. However, with the production of superplasticizers, these materials were also added to the constituents of self-compacting concrete. The above compounds require specialized and controlled concreting methods to prevent the separation and decomposition of concrete particles. In the early cases, the high amount of cement paste exposes the self-compacting concrete to concrete shrinkage, turning it into concrete with very high production costs and limited applications. In 1983, poor compaction and complete compression were recognized as the main cause of poor performance of concrete structures in Japan. Following the introduction of a new type of self-leveling concrete, or in other words, self-compacting concrete in this country, a new movement began with the aim of producing high quality concrete[4]

Since there was no practical possibility to ensure concrete compaction at the site, the main focus of the research was on removing the compaction agent by vibration or any other means. This led to the development of the first type of self-compacting concrete by two researchers, Okamura and Ozawa, in 1986 at the University of Tokyo. [4]

In 1994, five European organizations (Prefabricated Concrete Organization, Cement Association, Prepared Concrete Organization, Concrete Additives Production Federation and Concrete and Chemical Systems Specialization Manufacturing Federation) came together to develop advanced systems and materials for the manufacture and use of concrete. These organizations formed the European Design Team to visit the best recent work covering all aspects of self-compacting concrete. This document, called the

European Guidelines for Self-Compacting Concrete, has done a great service to European-accepted standards and testing methods. [1]

Self-compacting concrete is often produced with a low water-to-cement ratio in order to achieve high initial strength, faster removal from the formwork and faster use in elements and buildings. From the point of view of compressive strength, self-compacting concrete is often produced with low water to cement ratios in order to achieve high strength. [1]

1-2-1 11-year analysis of self-compacting concrete samples

In one study, 68 studies of the use of self-compacting concrete from 1993 to 2003 were reviewed and compared [6], which is one of the most widely used periods of consumption of these materials. To examine the reasons for using self-compacting concrete in 51 cases that are in executive projects, it is as follows:

1- It has been used in 34 cases (67%) due to its technical advantage over conventional vibrating concretes. In these projects, vibration during fuel has been very difficult or impossible due to high density of reinforcements or lack of access.

2. In seven cases (14%), a group of large Japanese contractors such as Kajimako, Mandako, and TC Group quickly absorbed the idea due to economic considerations and cost savings associated with the implementation time. The contractors used the facilities and equipment within their R&D unit to expand their compact concrete production technology. Each company designed its own composition for the production of self-compacting concrete and taught its employees how to use self-compacting concrete on construction sites like technical technicians. [4]

One of the most important issues in the development of self-compacting concrete was the expansion of laboratory equipment and test methods by large contractors. In the early 1990s, there was only one restriction on the dissemination of public information about self-compacting concrete, and that was the availability of information only in Japanese. In the same decade, keeping technical and basic information confidential by a large company in order to maintain business privileges was another problem. In the following years, self-compacting concrete under the brand names NVC (non-vibrated concrete) was used by Kajima company or high quality concrete SQC by Maeda company or Biocrete by TC company. [4] Simultaneously with the progress of Japanese companies in the field of self-compacting concrete, research in this field continued and research in this field continued, and new studies in composite designs and underwater concreting for the production of high quality concrete by Japanese companies Done. [4] and labor wages were used.

3- In five cases (10%) it has been used specifically in new structural elements such as steel-concrete composites and thin-walled prefabricated components.

4- In the remaining five cases, the reasons for use are either unclear or not stated. In some cases, environmental issues such as noise and vibration have also been effective in selecting these materials. [6]

1-2-1-1 New features

Flow drops, which are commonly used to measure flow, were also used in studies. Therefore, the amount of current loss in all samples is presented, which in about 50% of cases show an average between 650 to 700 mm and about 90% have an average of about 600 to 700 mm. There is no suitable model for the relationship between flow loss and mental velocity, which indicates the independence of these two features from each other and both should be considered in the design [6]. (Figure 1-1)

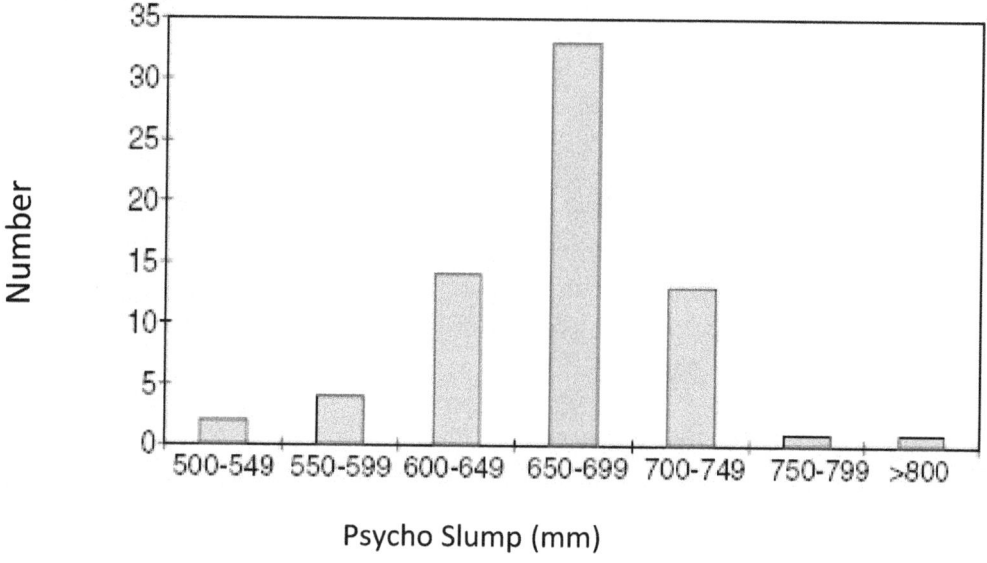

(Figure 1-1) Psychopath slump for the studied samples [6]

1-2-1-2 Compressive strength

In all the studied samples of 28-day compressive strength test, the amount of compressive strength in these experiments varies between 20 to 100 MPa and 80% of the resistance compounds have shown more than 40 MPa. (Figure 1-2)

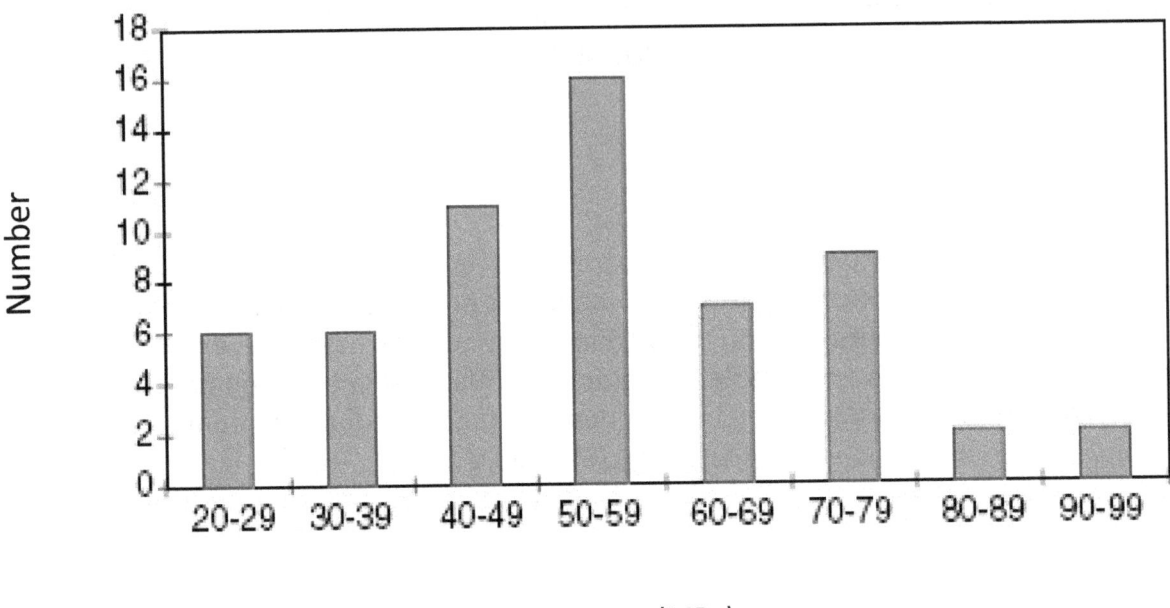

(Figure 1-2) 28-day resistance for the studied samples [6]

This proves the fact that the possibility of producing self-compacting concrete can be produced in almost any strength that ordinary concretes have. The amount of cement is the determining factor in strength and like ordinary concrete, the amount of water to cement is not the determining factor [6].

1-2-1-3 Compounds and components

Crushed stone has been used three times as much as sand, which indicates the availability of this material. Light aggregates have been used in two samples. 48 samples (approximately 70%) used particles with a thickness of 16 to 20% mm. The amount of coarse or fine-grained use depends on environmental factors. In 6 samples, particles with a thickness of 40 mm were used. Aggregates between 10-15 mm were used in 10 samples of studies. In all Except for 2 samples, a combination of Portland cement with one or two additional compounds (mixed or additive) was used. In 19 cases, a triple compound was used and in three cases, a quaternary compound was used. The justification for choosing the type of powder composition is to reduce the hydration temperature or to reduce the compressive strength.In more than half of the studies, more than 30% of the powdered form was added to the main mixture as a mixed additive. Viscosity agent is used that the reason for using this material is to create resistance to separation and reduce the sensitivity of concrete to changes in materials during the production process.

1-2-1-4 mixing ratio

1- Since coarse grains are covered by layers of mortar paste and, consequently, the flow rate of increasing the separation diameter of concrete particles decreases, coarse-grained compounds are used to a small extent.

2- By limiting the amount of fine particles and the ratio of water to powder and adding super-lubricants and viscosity modifiers, the desired fluidity and viscosity can be obtained. The results of self-compacting concrete mixing analysis in comparison with conventional concrete mixing show the following.

1- Less amount of coarse grains.
2- Increasing the amount of cement.
3- High volume of powdered materials.
4- Lower ratio of water to powdered materials.
5- High amount of superplasticizer.
6- Using viscous (in some cases)

Therefore, the following items were selected for the design of self-compacting concrete mixing.

1- Coarse grain amount (based on volume)
2- Amount of cement (based on volume)
3- The amount of powder compounds (based on weight)
4- Ratio of water to powder materials (based on weight)
5- The volume of fine particles to the volume of mortar

1-2-1-5 Amounts of materials

Depending on the volume of concrete, the amount of coarse grain varies between 28 to 38%, which is approximately equivalent to 725-925 kg / m3. The amount of cement varies from 30 to 42% depending on the volume of concrete. The amount of powder material varies between 425 to 625 kg / m3. The average of powder particles in 80% of the samples varies between 0.28 and 0.42. The ratio of water to powder materials has a very important effect on the hardness and freshness of self-compacting concrete and the amount of powder has a more important effect on the hydration process, the amount of heat and the final strength. There is a clear difference between viscous compounds and those that do not. During the research on self-compacting concrete, the mixtures are divided into three groups based on the amount of plastic viscosity required to prevent separation:

1- Powder types: ratio of water to cement, low amount of powder, high dose of superplasticizer.

2- Types of viscosity modifiers: High water to cement ratio A significant amount of more viscosity modifiers has been used for underwater concretes.

3- Combined types: This category is a combination of the previous two types and is designed with quantities that have a low water to cement ratio and a viscous modifier. [6]

Mortar composition in the form of fine-grained volume of the whole mortar varies from 28% to 54%. In 80% of the samples, these values vary between 41% and 52%. The initial mixing design process proposed in the early years of the use of viscosity modifiers for the production of good mixtures suggested a value of 40%, which recent studies show is a high value.

1-2-1-6 Properties of the mixture

Coarse-grained cement and the fine-grained percentage of mortar are all approximately 20%. While the amount of powder and the ratio of water to powder is much higher. (32% and 42%, respectively). The first three ratios can be used to obtain a good self-compacting concrete, while the next two ratios affect the greater flexibility of the concrete.

1-2-2 Execution examples of self-compacting concrete [7]

Various structures in the world have been constructed using self-compacting concrete, examples of which we will mention. It is noteworthy that some of these projects could not have been implemented without the use of self-compacting concrete.

1- Akashi-Kaiko suspension bridge

The length of the bridge was originally designed to be 3,910 meters, but the great Hanshin earthquake on January 17, 1995 increased the length by one meter. (Figure 1-3)
Span length = 1991 meters.
Volume of self-compacting concrete consumption = 290,000 cubic meters.
Distance of self-compacting concrete through pipes and pumping = about 200 meters.
Length of cables used in suspension bridge = 300000 km.

Bridge construction cost = $ 4.3 billion.
Savings in construction time = about 20% (about 2.5-2 years of time savings) compared to conventional concrete.

(Figure 1-3) Akashi-Kaiko suspension bridge

2- The walls of the huge LNG tanks of Japan Osaka Gas Company[7]

Volume of self-compacting concrete consumption = 12000 cubic meters (with high strength of 60 Newtons per square millimeter). (Figure 1-4)

Savings in the number of workers = about 67% (from 150 to 50 people) compared to ordinary concrete.

Savings in construction time = about 18% (from 22 months to 18 months) compared to conventional concrete.

Saving the number of workshops = about 29% from 14 workshops to 10 workshops compared to ordinary concrete.

(Figure 1-4) first LNG tank walls

3- Midsummer Place, located in London, England. [8]

Elliptical columns with very dense rebars with a height of 10-5 / 8 meters. (Figure 1-5)
Project value = 65 million £.
Save time = about 40% compared to conventional concrete.
Cost savings = about 10% compared to conventional concrete.

(Figure 1-5) Midsummer Place

4- Immersed tunnel project in Kobe, Japan. [8]

In this project, self-compacting concrete is used in another form, which is called sandwich structures. (Figure 1-6)
In this type of structures, self-compacting concrete is filled in steel shells. It should be noted that this project could not have been implemented without the use of self-compacting concrete.

(Figure 1-6) Submersible tunnel project in Kobe, Japan

5- Landmark Tower in Yokohama, Japan. [9]

The tallest tower in Japan with a height of 295.8 meters and 70 floors. (Figure 1-7)
The columns of the first 9 floors of the tower are made of dense concrete (due to the compactness of the rebars).
Number of 9-story columns = 66 columns.
Amount of self-compacting concrete consumption = 885 cubic meters.

(Figure 1-7) Landmark Tower

Bunkers hill project in Calgary, western Canada, which is one of the largest commercial and administrative projects in Canada. Self-compacting concrete is used in two radii-type foundations, construction of two residential tower units in Nantes, France, renovation of Schniech tunnel (concrete itself Density resistant to frost and ice melting, less shrinkage compared to ordinary concrete as surface concrete in concrete walls), construction of Alp Guttard tunnel (use of concrete spraying system, sulfate-resistant self-compacting concrete, impermeable) Hotel development Crowne Plaza and other examples of the use of self-compacting concrete in Switzerland. (Figure 1-8)

(Figure 1-8) Crowne Plaza Hotel [10]

Chapter Two
Definitions and review of research

2-1 Definitions

2-1-1 Mineral additives
They are very fine minerals that are used to improve certain properties or to achieve special properties in concrete. The Federation of Specialized Construction of Concrete and Chemical Systems has dealt with two types of micronutrients.
1- Almost neutral additive (type one)
2- Latent hydraulic additive or pozzolan (type two)

2-1-2 Chemical additives
Materials that are added during the mixing of concrete. The amount of these materials is small and depends on the amount of cement and is used to modify some properties of fresh or hardened concrete.

2-1-3 Adhesive
The combination of cement and hydraulic additive in a self-compacting concrete is called adhesive [9].

2-1-4 Filling capability (unlimited flow capability)
The ability of self-compacting concrete to flow inward and completely fill all the spaces between the formwork, under its own weight.

2-1-5 Mortar
The part of concrete that contains cement paste, plus aggregates smaller than 4 mm.

2-1-6 Cement paste
Part of concrete that contains cement powder plus weather.

2-1-7 Passability (limited flow capability)
The ability of self-compacting concrete to flow through narrow paths such as the space between steel reinforcements without separation or blockage.

2-1-8 Powder (fine material)
Fine materials in sizes smaller than 0.125 mm. The powder can also contain some sand in this size.

2-1-9 Self-compacting concrete

Concrete that is able to flow under its own weight and, without the need for vibration, completely fills the formwork even with dense reinforcement, while maintaining its homogeneity.

2-1-10 Resistance to separation (stability)

Ability of self-compacting concrete to maintain its structure homogeneously during transport and concreting [11].

2-1-11 Efficiency

Ease of concreting and compacting fresh concrete, which is a complex combination of fluidity, adhesion, portability, compressibility and viscosity.

2-1-12 Chemical additives

Superplasticizers are an essential component in self-compacting concrete to achieve the required performance. Other additives used in compacted concrete include viscosity modifiers, which are used to increase durability, and aerobics, which are used to increase frost resistance [11].

2-1-13 Mineral additives

Because of the special rheological properties required in self-compacting concrete, both active and inactive additives are used to improve performance, regulate pressure, and reduce hydration heat.

2-1-13-1 Types of mineral additives

1- Stone powder: Dolomite, granite and limestone that have been eaten very finely may be used as powder. Particles smaller than 0.125 mm can be useful.

Note: Dolomite may pose a risk to the durability of concrete due to the alkaline carbonate reaction.

2-Wind ash: It is a very fine mineral with pozzolanic properties that is added to it to improve the properties of its compacted concrete.

3-Silica fume: has a favorable effect on the rheological properties of compacted concrete. It also improves the durability of concrete [11].

2-1-14 Powder for melting iron

Melting iron powder has very fine grains and hidden hydraulic properties which, if used in self-compacting concrete, improves its rheological properties [11].

2-1-15 Glass filler powder

The particle size of glass filler powder is less than 0.1 mm and its specific surface area is larger than 2500 square centimeters per gram. Larger grains may cause an alkaline silica reaction [11].

2-1-16 Pigment

Suitable pigments for use in self-compacting concrete are listed in European Regulation.

2-1-17 Fibers

Fibers are used to improve self-compacting concrete Like conventional concrete, steel fibers are used to enhance the mechanical properties of concrete, such as flexural strength and hardness.
Polymer fibers are used to reduce plastic detachment and creep or to increase fire resistance.
For ease in the mixing and concreting steps, it is recommended that the tests be performed on site and approved by the supervising engineer [11].

2.2 Fresh self-compacting concrete tests

In the case of self-compacting concrete, the three parameters of filling capacity, permeability and separation resistance must be measured.
These three parameters are not always independent of each other and are related to each other to varying degrees. The viscosity component, which is affected by the filling ability, is closely related to the degree of separation resistance.
The ability to pass is also affected by factors such as the composition of stone materials, ductility, resistance to detachment and the conditions of structures in which concrete is used.
There are several different tests to determine the characteristics of self-compacting concrete. The reason for this is that a fixed test method alone can not accurately show all the characteristics of compacted concrete [11]. Also, a test method can not record the performance of self-compacting concrete because there are different factors that have different effects on the performance of this concrete.
The proposed test methods for self-compacting concrete are given in Tables 1-2 and 2.2.

(Table 2-1) List of test methods for determining the properties of self-compacting concrete [11]

Testing method	Specifications
Slump flow	Filling capability
Slump flow time 50 cm	Filling capacity
Ring J Figure	Passability
Funnel V Figure	Filling capability
Increase V-shaped funnel time 5 minutes	Detachment resistance
L-shaped mold	Passability
U-shape	passability
Orimet	Filling Capability

(Table 2-2) Acceptance criteria for self-compacting concrete [11]

Test methods	limited in results	
	Minimum	Maximum
Slump current (mm)	650	800
Slump flow time up to 50 cm (s)	2	5
J-shaped ring (mm)	0	10
V-shaped funnel (seconds)	6	12
Increase V-shaped funnel time in five minutes (seconds)	0	3
L-shaped format (ratio h2 / h1)	0.8	1
U-shaped h2- h1 (mm)	0	30
Orimet (seconds)	0	5

2-2-1 Slump flow test and slump flow time up to 50 cm

The main rheological parameters of self-compacting concrete are plastic viscosity and yield value, which determine the filling capacity of self-compacting concrete. Slump current and slump flow time up to 50 cm show a good relationship with these parameters that have good reproducibility [12].

Slump test is one of the most common tests to measure the properties of compacted concrete and the reason for this is the process of doing it and the equipment used is relatively simple. This test demonstrates the ability of concrete to fill.

The test method is similar to the slump test method. The diameter of the concrete circle is a measure of the filling capacity of concrete (Figure 2-2).

If we want to measure the slump flow time up to 50 cm, two people are needed to perform the experiment. This test can be easily done in the workshop, although the plate under the concrete is large and heavy [11].

The flow time of 500 mm (flow time from the initial diameter of 200 mm to 500 mm) or the final flow time of (when the slump cone is removed until the flow stops) is usually considered to evaluate the viscosity of fresh concrete.

The final flow time of concrete is more affected by the final flow rate of slump and human judgment than the flow time of 500 mm. Therefore, a flow time of 500 mm is more useful for evaluating the viscosity of the compound. However, the flow time of 500 mm is also affected by the amount of slump current (deformation capacity).

For example, when the viscosity of the composition is constant, the slump current of most concrete leads to a flow time of 500 mm lower.

2-2-1-1 Experimental steps

About six liters of concrete is required for the test. Wet the bottom plate and the inner surface of the slump cone. Place the bottom plate in a flat place and place the slump cone on it and in the center. Fill the cone with a whisk. Avoid hitting and shaking the cone and level the concrete surface with the butt of the cone. We clean the poured concrete around the cone. Pull the slip cone up vertically and allow the concrete to flow. Simultaneously with lifting the cone, we measure the stopwatch and measure the time when the concrete reaches a circle with a diameter of 50 cm. (This time is the slump flow time up to 50 cm).

We measure the diameter of a circle in two perpendicular directions. We calculate the average of the two measured diameters. (Qatar obtained gives us the flow of Islam) [11].

2-2-1-2 Interpretation of results

The higher the slump flow, the greater the concrete's ability to fill the mold under its own weight. A value of at least 650 mm is suitable for self-compacting concrete.

Time to reach a diameter of 50 cm is the second sign of flow. Less time indicates better flow capability. Research has shown that a time of 3-7 seconds is acceptable for civil engineering work and a time of 2-5 seconds is acceptable for a building.

Slump testing is one of the easiest ways to measure the resistance to separation of fresh self-compacting concrete by visual observation. When separation resistance is not sufficient, coarse aggregates tend to be in the center. However, visual observation is not suitable for quantitative estimation. (Figure 2-1)

(Figure 2-1) Slump test

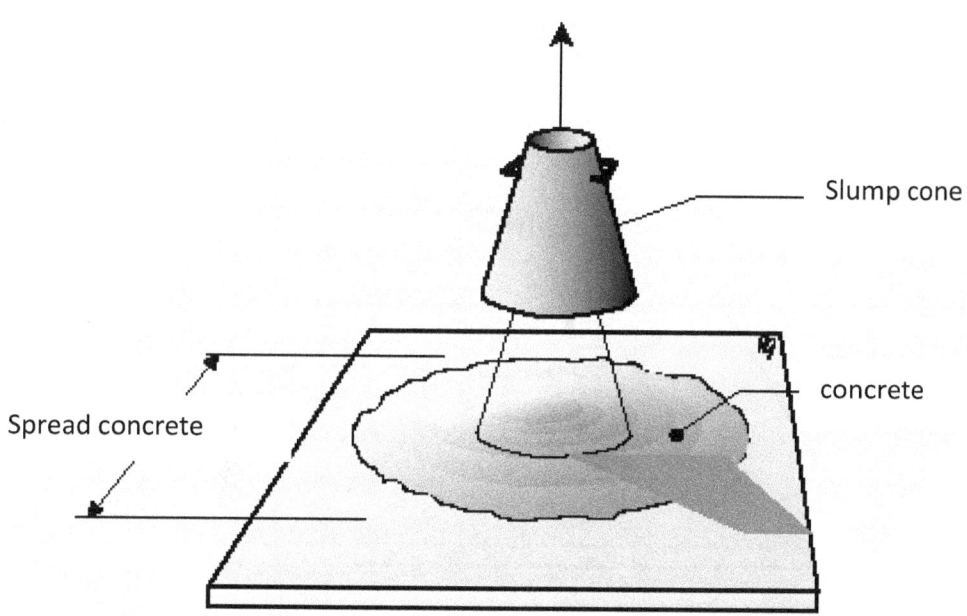

(Figure 2-2) Slump test machine [2]

26

When severe separation occurs, coarse aggregates remain in the center of the circle and mortar and cement paste move out of the circle. When low separation occurs, a boundary of coarse aggregate-free mortar is formed on the outside [11].

2-2-2 J-shaped ring test

This is probably the first time the experiment has been performed by the Japanese, but there is no reference. This test is used for passability.

To perform the test, we need a steel plate on which the reinforcements are mounted vertically. The reinforcements are located on a circle in the center of the plate and the diameter and distance of the reinforcements from each other can be different. The distance between the rebars can be three times the maximum size of the aggregate. The diameter of the circle on which the rebars are located is 300 mm and the height of the rebars is 100 mm (Figure 2-3).

The J-shaped loop test can be used in addition to the slump flow tests, the orifice test and the V-shaped funnel. These tests show the permeability and flowability of concrete. After the test, the height of the concrete inside and outside the ring is measured. The results show the permeability and the rate of passage of concrete through enclosed reinforcements [11]. (Figure 2-4)

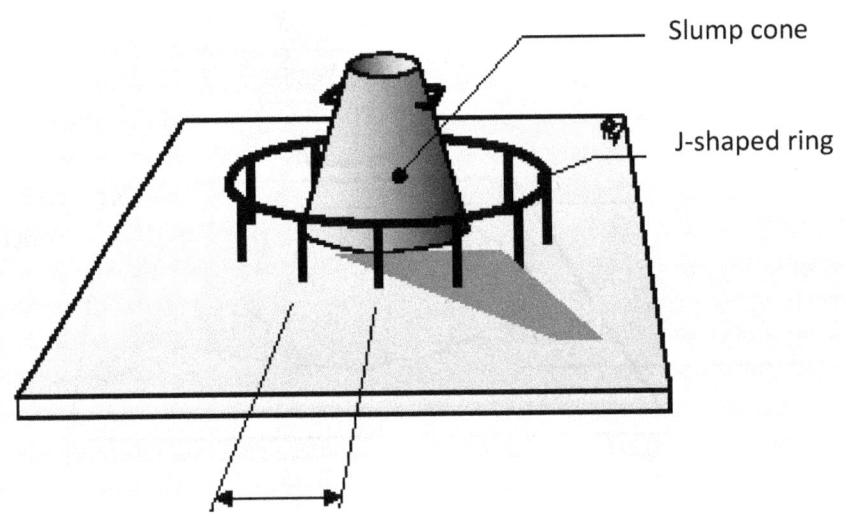

The space between the gaps

(Figure 2-3) J-shaped ring

(Figure 2-4) J-ring loop test [4] [24].

2.2.3 Test the V-shaped funnel and increase the time of the V-shaped funnel in five minutes

This experiment was proposed in Japan by Ozawa [13]. A V-shaped funnel according to Figure 2-5 is required to perform the test.

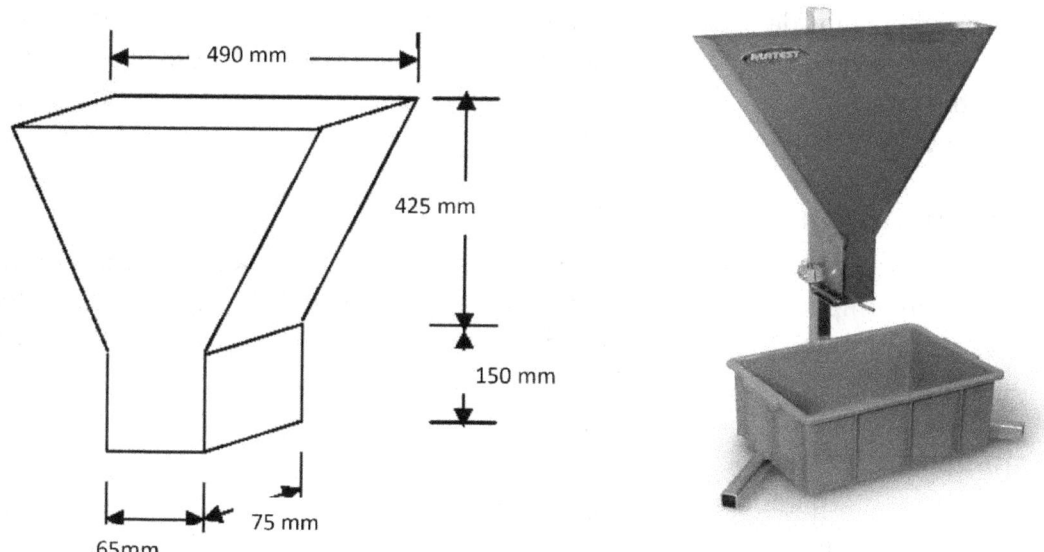

Figure 2-5) V-shaped funnel [5].

This test to some extent indicates the ability to fill and block that can be easily used both in the workshop and in the laboratory [14]. It is not used for concretes containing aggregates with a diameter of more than 25 mm.

The hopper is filled with approximately 12 liters of concrete, then the valve is opened and the discharge time of the concrete is measured with a stopwatch.

Then refill the funnel with concrete and allow it to settle for five minutes. If the concrete separates, the funnel emptying time will increase.

The high discharge time can be due to the high viscosity of the mortar or the high friction between the aggregates.

2-2-3-1 Experimental steps

About 12 liters of concrete is required for the test. Place the funnel in a fixed place. Wet the surface inside the mold. Open the valve to remove excess water. After the excess water comes out, close the valve and place the bucket under it.

Pour the concrete into the funnel without vibration or impact and raise the concrete surface to the top edge of the funnel. Ten seconds after filling the funnel, open the valve so that the concrete flows under its own weight.

We close the stopwatch at the same time as opening the valve and measure the time of complete emptying of the concrete. Then we perform the test of increasing the time of the V-shaped funnel in five minutes.

The steps for increasing the time of the V-shaped funnel in five minutes are as follows:

Do not clean or wet the inside of the funnel. Close the funnel lid and refill the inside. Place the bucket under the valve. We smooth the upper surface of the concrete. Five minutes after refilling the hopper, open the valve and allow the concrete to flow. The discharge time of the funnel is measured with a stopwatch.

2-2-3-2 Interpretation of test results

This test measures the ease of concrete flow. Less flow time indicates more flow capability. For self-compacting concrete, a flow rate of 10 seconds is appropriate. After five minutes, the separation shows its effect more and as a result, the flow time increases [11].

2-2-4 L-shaped mold test

In this experiment, the flow of concrete and the role of concrete blockage due to the presence of rebars are shown. The shape of the mold is shown in Figure 2-16.

The mold consists of a vertical section and a horizontal rectangular section separated by a movable valve.

It is placed in the outlet of vertical reinforcements. The vertical part of the formwork is filled with concrete, then the valve is pulled upwards and the concrete flows in the horizontal part.

When the flow stops, we obtain the ratio of the height of the concrete at the end of the horizontal section to the height of the remaining concrete inside the vertical section, which indicates the permeability and the amount of concrete passing through the enclosing reinforcements.

The valve is marked on the horizontal part of the formwork at intervals of 20 and 40 cm, to measure how long it takes for the concrete to travel the above distances. These numbers are indicated by the symbols T40 and T50 and indicate the filling capacity.

The diameter of the rebars can be different and can be placed at different distances. When tested with conventional reinforcements, the distance between the reinforcements up to three times the size of the largest aggregate is appropriate. This test is suitable for the laboratory and perhaps the workshop and shows the ability to fill and pass its own compacted concrete.

2-2-4-1 Experimentation steps

About 14 liters of concrete is required to perform the test. Place the mold on a flat, stable surface to ensure proper valve operation. Moisten the inner surface of the mold and clean excess water. While the valve is closed, we fill the vertical part of the mold with concrete. After one minute, open the sliding valve and allow the concrete to flow. . At the same time as opening the valve, we also hit the stopwatch and note the times T40 and T20. When the concrete stops moving, we measure the heights of H2 and H1. We calculate the H2 / H1 ratio.

2-2-4-2 Interpretation of results

If the concrete flows like water then the value is H2 / H1 = 1.
The minimum value of H2 / H1 accepted by the European standard is 0.8.
The times T40 and T20 indicate ease of flow.
Obstruction of coarse aggregates next to reinforcements is also easily detectable [11]. (Figure 2-7)

(Figure 2-6) L-shaped mold

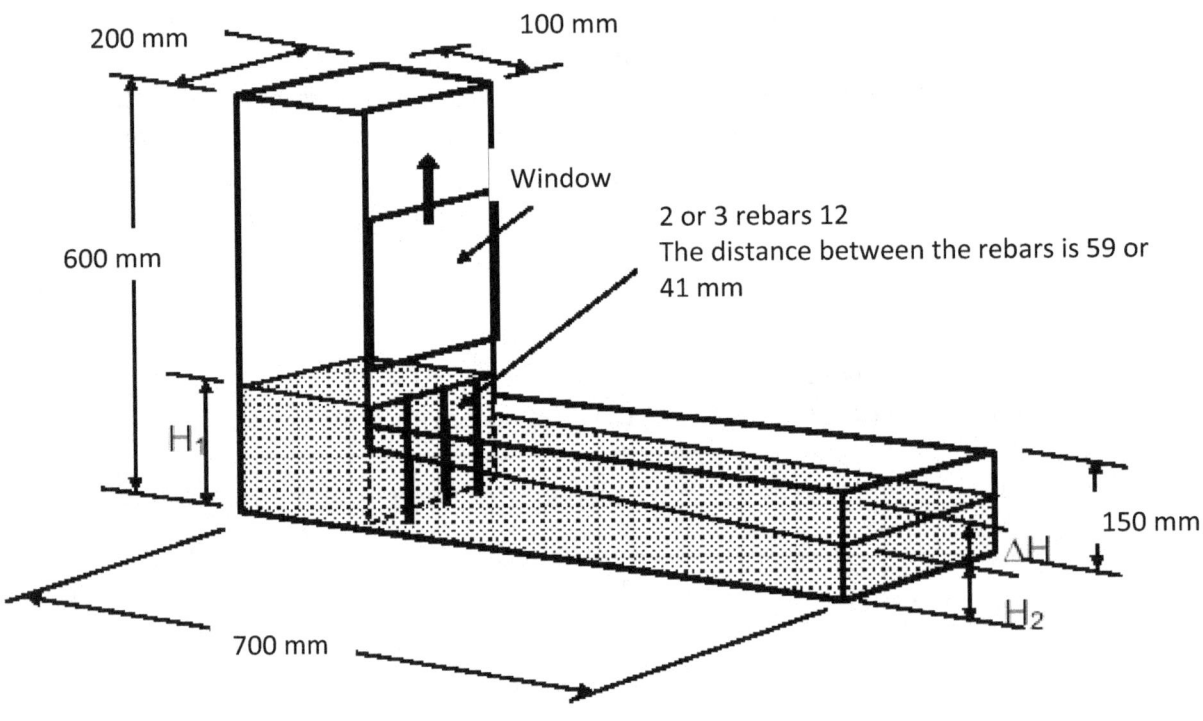

(Figure 2-7) L-Box device [22]

31

Except in special cases, the results of this test are well consistent with the results of the slump test. That is, it indicates the capacity for deformation. The height drop of the sample has a similar physical meaning to the amount of slump. In other words, the slump flow test measures the two-dimensional flow ability of concrete specimens under free conditions, and the L-shaped mold test evaluates the one-dimensional flow ability (under one-way reinforcement conditions). However, in cases where the concrete sample has a high tendency to detach or the amount of coarse aggregate in the composition is relatively high, it is possible to stop the movement of concrete by creating an obstruction in the opening valve. When such a phenomenon occurs, the results of the L-shaped template do not match the results of the slump.

A higher value of h (sample height drop) indicates the ability of better measured concrete to pass through narrow openings. The time to reach a certain distance (T40, T20) is used to evaluate the deformation speed.

Differences in height before and after the reinforcement table (obstruction ratio) are used to evaluate the ability to pass through narrow openings that include deformation capacity and obstruction properties.

2-2-5 U-shaped mold test

This test is used to measure the filling capacity of self-compacting concrete. The format of this experiment is a U-shaped container divided into two parts by a wall in the middle (Figure 2-8). There is also a sliding valve between the two parts. Reinforcements with a diameter of 13 mm with a center-to-center distance of 50 mm are placed at the valve, so the distance between the rebars is 35 mm.

The left side of the mold is filled with 20 liters of concrete and then the sliding valve is opened.

As soon as the hatch opens, the concrete moves upwards on the opposite side, then the height of the concrete is measured in both sections.

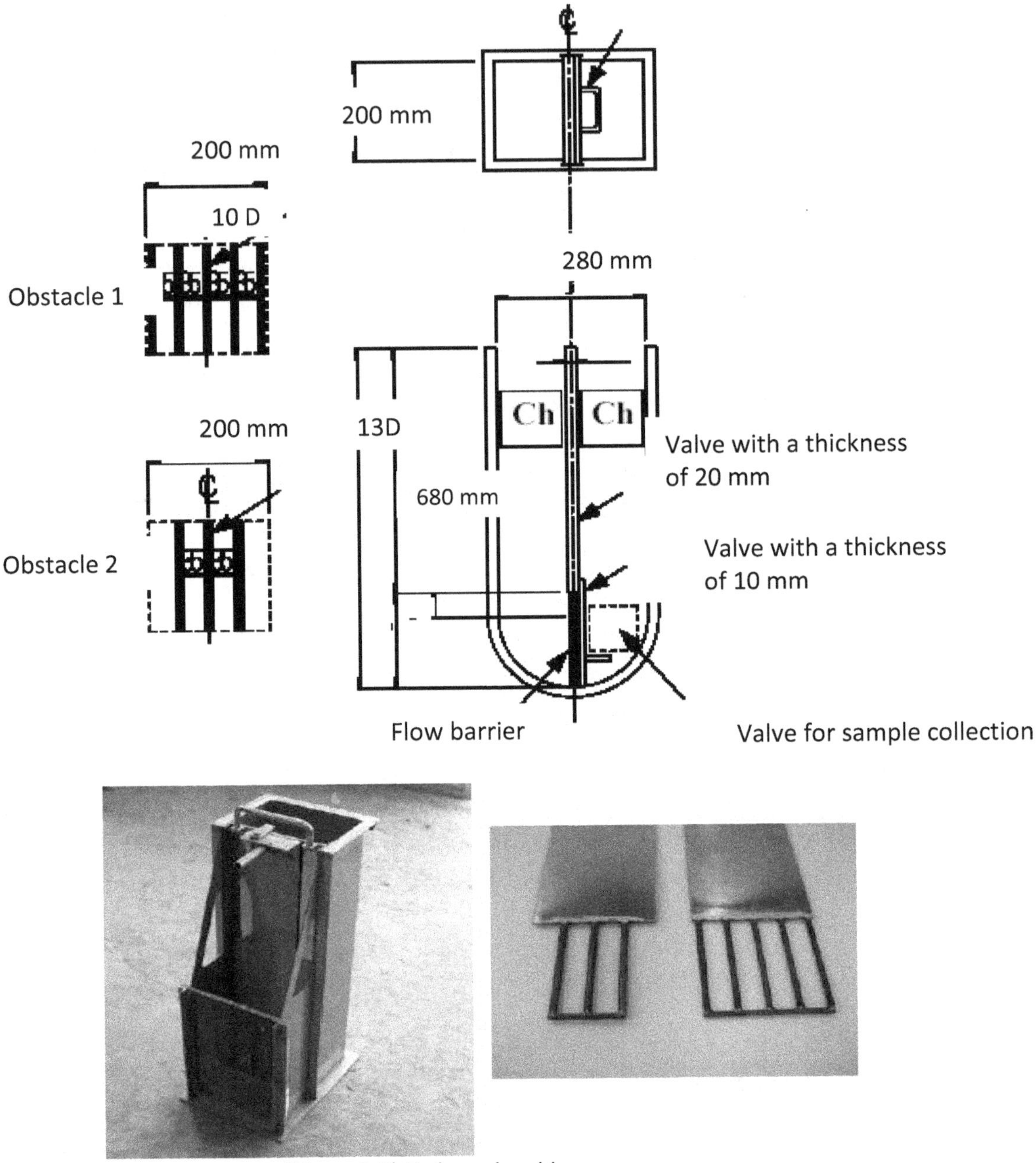

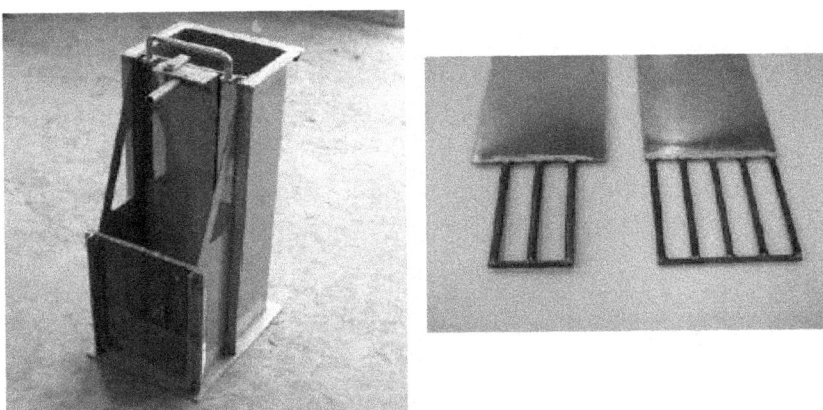

(Figure 2-8) U-shaped mold

2-2-5-1 Interpretation of results

When evaluating the results of this test, it should be noted that similar to the results of the V-shaped funnel test, the physical concept of filling height is affected by the components of the concrete composition being tested. For example, when the size and amount of coarse aggregate is small enough relative to the free distance between the installed reinforcement, the filling height is strongly related to the deformation capacity (slump flow rate) of the concrete sample.

Therefore, separation resistance is a very determining factor in the filling height.

In such an example, the flow time (flow velocity) indicates the viscosity of the compound, which controls the separation resistance.

On the other hand, when the size and amount of coarse grains are relatively large relative to the free distance of the installed reinforcement, the collision between the coarse grains has a significant effect on the ability to pass through narrow openings. In such a sample, the concrete with the possibility of detachment often has a low filling height. Even if the concrete has a high slump rate and the flow rate tends to decrease due to the impact of coarse aggregates. Even if the viscosity of the composition is not too high.

2-2-6 Fill box test 1

This test is also known as the Kajima 2 test.

This test is used to measure the filling capacity of self-compacting concrete with a maximum aggregate size of 20 mm [11].

Early in the development of self-compacting concrete, some types of filling box experiments were developed to model high-density reinforced structures on a small scale, and fresh concrete was used to evaluate self-compaction.

Figure 2-9 shows a typical example of such a device.

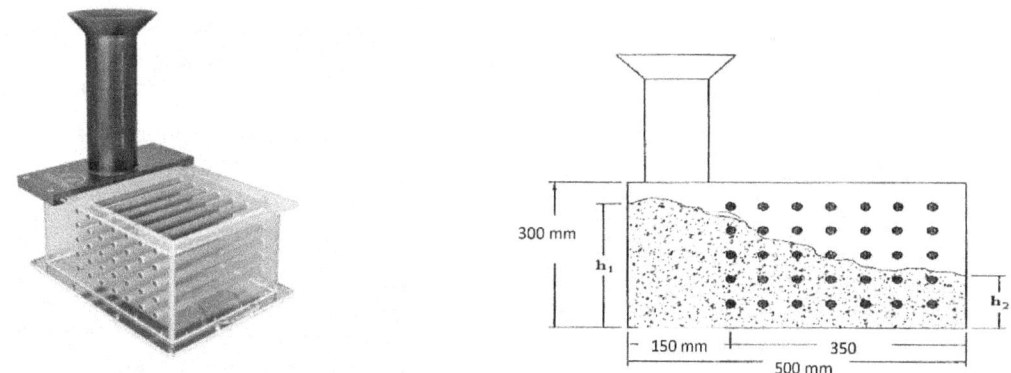

(Figure 2-9) Filling box test device [11]

This device includes a transparent box with smooth surfaces in which 35 barriers made of PVC with a diameter of 20 mm and a distance from the center to the center of 50 mm are installed (Figure 2-9).

At the top of the box, a tube with a diameter of 100 mm and a height of 50 mm, at the top of which there is a funnel with a height of 100 mm, is installed to fill the box. The inside of the box is filled with concrete with the help of pipes and funnels and the difference in concrete height on both sides of the box is measured, which indicates the ability of the concrete to be filled. It is difficult to perform this experiment in the workshop [11].

The biggest advantage of this method is the ease of viscosity of fresh concrete. Judging whether a compacted concrete is good or bad can be made clearly by the flow behavior and filling of the poured concrete.

The purpose of this experiment is to simultaneously determine the ability to pass through narrow openings and the ability to self-compact. By changing the size of the free distance between the reinforcements, the balance between these two properties can be controlled. The concrete sample gradually fills and the previously poured concrete moves due to the pressure of the next poured concrete. In a sample where pre-cast concrete is stuck due to insufficient ability to pass through narrow valves, the new concrete passes over the previous concrete. The motion of the concrete is similar to the actual visible conditions and this is the advantage of this type of test.

2-2-7 Sieve Stability Test

This test is used to determine the resistance to separation. In this test, about 10 liters of concrete is placed in a covered container for 15 minutes (in order to prevent any internal separation). Then about two liters of the sample is poured into a container. Then the concrete is poured from a height of 500 mm on sieve number 4 with a diameter of 350 mm and after two minutes the percentage of weight passing through the sieve is calculated (r). According to the recommendation of the Federation of Specialized Construction of Concrete and Chemical Systems 2, the allowable range r is considered between 0 and 15% [11].

2-2-8 Orimet method

This method was developed in Kashmir University to determine the efficiency of fresh concrete with high fluency in construction workshops [11]. Required supplies are shown in Figure 2-7. Erimat consists of a vertical cast iron pipe that is fastened to an inverted cone and a valve is used to close the hole. Usually the inner diameter of the valve is 80 mm and the maximum aggregate size is limited to 20 mm.

(*Figure 2-10*) *Orimet device [12]*

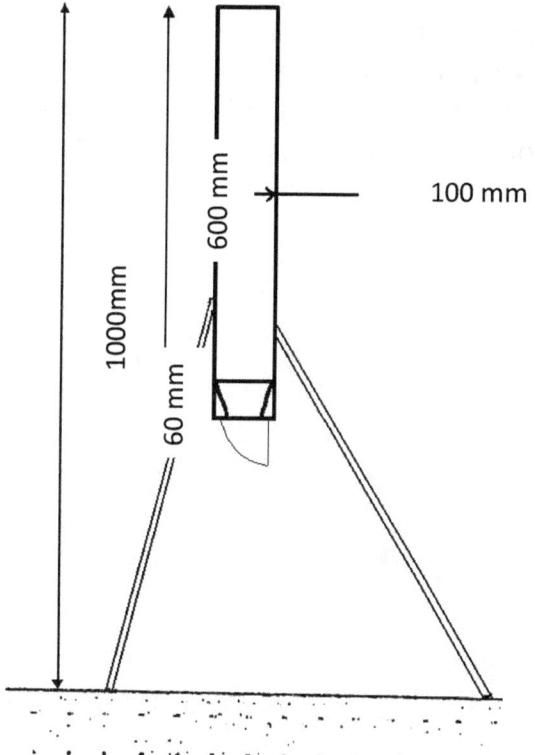

(*Figure 2-10*) *Erimat device [11]*

This test shows the fluidity of concrete during the concrete road in the workshop and is a quick test method with simple tools.

2-2-8-1 Interpretation of results

The test calculates the mental discharge, the less discharge time is more psychological equivalent, for self-compacting concrete the discharge time of five seconds and less is desirable.

2-2-9 Session column method

Resistance to separation is also provided by the column. As shown in Figure 2-11.
The dimensions used for the test are 100-150-500 mm. Concrete is poured into the tester. A cycle of controlled blows enters the device. After a period of time for standard sitting, test specimens are taken from the top and bottom of the device through built-in valves [15].
These samples are examined by determining the amount of coarse grains. The ratio between the coarse mass in the sample taken from the top to the coarse mass in the sample taken from the end is the expression of heat resistance against separation. The lower ratio indicates more coarse grains in the lower layers and therefore, the greater the tendency to detach.

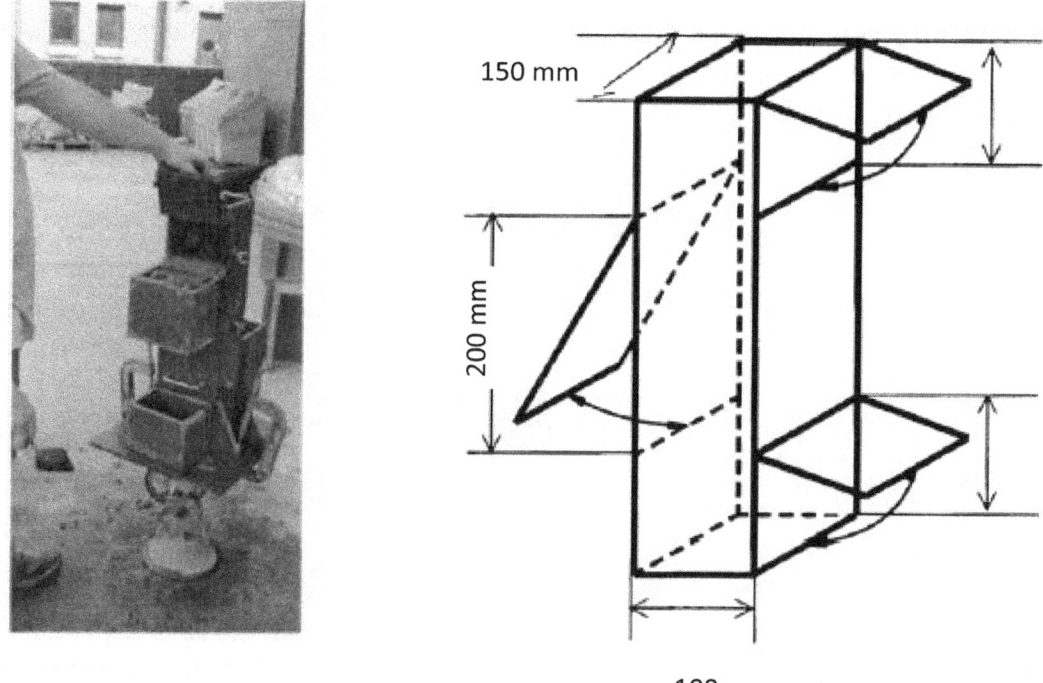

(Figure 2-11) Sitting column test machine [15]

In some sources [16] other tests have been mentioned such as pumping capability, surface polishing capability, plastic settling, washing resistance [16]. Which is not common and exact information on how to perform these tests is not available.

2-3 tests performed

2-3-1 Test to determine the resistance of concrete to ice cycle and ice melting

This test involves determining the strength of concrete against rapid and successive freezing and thawing cycles. This experiment intends to investigate the effects of changes in the properties and conditions of concrete on the strength of self-compacting concrete against solidification and melting cycles performed in a particular method. This test is performed in the laboratory in two ways:

Method A: Freezing and rapid melting in water.
Method B: Rapid freezing in air and melting in water.

Both methods are used to determine the effect of changes in the properties and conditions of concrete resistance to freezing and thawing cycles with a special method.

It should be noted that when the sample of method A is under test of thawing and freezing, it should be kept in water between 1 to 3 mm in vertical containers. .

This test means that the ice and ice melting test was performed in accordance with ASTM C666, which is described in detail in the following chapters.

2-3-2 Alkaline silica reaction test

This experiment is an accelerated method to investigate the alkaline silica reaction potential of aggregate in mortar. Due to the fact that in this particular concrete, in addition to cement, filler (fly ash) has also been used, so this experiment was performed to investigate the effect of alkaline silica reaction on the strength of self-compacting concrete.

The accelerated alkaline silica test is performed in accordance with ASTM C1260 as described in Chapter 4.

2-4 Rheology self-compacting concrete

Mixed rheology means viscosity and flowability, as well as its susceptibility to blockage and separation [2].

This type of concrete is very popular and has a wide range of benefits, especially in conditions with hard formwork such as sections with dense reinforcement. Compacted concrete is defined as concrete that shows high ductility and good resistance to separation. . The use of viscous additives along with superplasticizers can lead to high ductility and good stability.

Superplasticizer significantly increases the performance of self-compacting concrete and reduces the amount of water as much as possible. [15] The cement paste must be sufficiently fluid to ensure the fluidity of the concrete itself and viscous enough to hold the coarse grains. In fact, since non-zero shear yield stress is able to prevent separation, viscosity is able to limit its effects. Therefore, understanding the rheological behavior of fresh self-compacting concrete mortars is the first step to studying the basic properties in the stability of self-compacting concrete.

2-4-1 Performance of self-compacting concrete

In order to achieve spontaneous compaction, both the ductility of the paste or mortar must be high and there must be sufficient resistance to coarse-grained and mortar separation when the concrete is flowing in the area enclosed by the reinforcing mesh.

Self-compacting requires the satisfaction of the following tasks for fresh concrete.

1- Filling ability
2- Resistance to separation
3- Ability to pass

2-4-2 Filling capability

The viscosity of the paste in its compacted concrete is higher than the viscosity of the paste in other types of concrete and this is due to the lower ratio of water to powder in its compacted concrete. This feature is effective in preventing separation [4]

On the other hand, reducing the ratio of water to powder can limit the ability of cement paste to deform.

Therefore, the ratio of water to powder must be controlled, because too much or too little of this ratio leads to improper ductility. Dough with super-lubricant with very low water to powder ratio leads to high deformation capacity and low deformation rate.

Since self-compacting concrete must be able to deform or deform well under its own weight, it is important to note that the friction between solid particles (coarse-grained, fine-grained and all types of powders) must be reduced.

2-4-3 Separation resistance

Detachment of fresh concrete is caused by non-uniform distribution of its constituent materials. Under certain conditions, the concrete may not tend to separate, but in other conditions, such as passing through sections with a large amount of reinforcement, separation may occur.

In order to have adequate resistance to separation, the following steps must be taken:

1- Reducing the distance between solid particles

This is done by limiting the maximum grain size, reducing the grain size, reducing the water-to-powder ratio, and using viscosity modifiers.

2- Minimize dehydration

This is done through the use of low water, low water to powder ratio, high specific surface powder materials and the use of viscosity modifiers.

2-4-4 Crossing ability

Self-compacting concrete to have effective performance must have sufficient flexibility with adequate resistance to separation and in cases where the molds have narrow openings or are faced with high density of reinforcement, the formation of coarse aggregates in narrow openings To be prevented. Therefore, it is necessary to create a compatibility between the size and amount of large particles in the compacted concrete and the free distance between the reinforcements and the openings of the formwork through which the concrete must pass.

For self-compacting concrete with good filling ability and good resistance to separation, blockage occurs under the following conditions.

1- The maximum size of aggregate should be very large.
2- The amount of coarse aggregate is very high.
Therefore, to provide the ability to pass properly, the following measures should be considered
1- Increasing viscosity in order to reduce the separation of aggregates
2- Low water to powder ratio
In order to reduce the obstruction, a suitable compatibility between coarse aggregates and free distances should be considered. For this purpose, the following measures are effective.
1- Reducing the volume of coarse aggregates
2- Reducing the maximum size of aggregates
Some concretes require a high slump, which is easily achieved by adding superplasticizer to the concrete. In such concretes, in order to maintain sufficient adhesion during operation, special attention should be paid to the details of mixing.
A simple suggestion to avoid separation by adding superplasticizer is to increase the amount of sand relative to the coarse grain [5]. But by reducing the coarse grain in practice, a large volume of cement must be added, which leads to an increase in hydration temperature and an increase in cost. The use of fly ash also improves the psychological properties and reduces concrete cracks due to the hydration heat of the cement [5].

Chapter Three

A variety of methods for determining the strength of concrete in situ

3- Types of methods for determining the strength of concrete in situ

Determining the strength of concrete after construction of concrete structures is very necessary to use the test results to determine the strength of concrete and the favorable or unfavorable operating conditions and damage to the structure due to changes in load (due to change of use) Evaluated. Various methods for testing concrete in structures have been developed, which can be divided into the following three groups:

1- Non-destructive group.
2- Semi-destructive group.
3- Destructive group.

3-1 Non-destructive tests

3-1-1 Ultrasonic wave velocity test

Ultrasonic wave velocity is affected by the elastic and mechanical properties of concrete. Therefore, a change in wave velocity along the path indicates a change in the quality of the concrete. Changes in the structure of concrete due to resistance or damage can increase or decrease the velocity of the waves. Also, the actual specific gravity and the specific gravity are completely compacted and the resulting strength is closely related. Therefore, by increasing the ratio of water to cement, the specific gravity and compressive strength decrease and the speed of the waves decreases. [17]

Relationship between wave velocity and strength of concrete under the influence of various factors such as age of concrete, processing conditions, moisture content, size of aggregates, type of aggregate and cement, temperature, microcracks and. . . is. Calibration curves for an assumed concrete exist experimentally, and with this method the compressive strength can be obtained in the most favorable conditions with an accuracy of 20%.

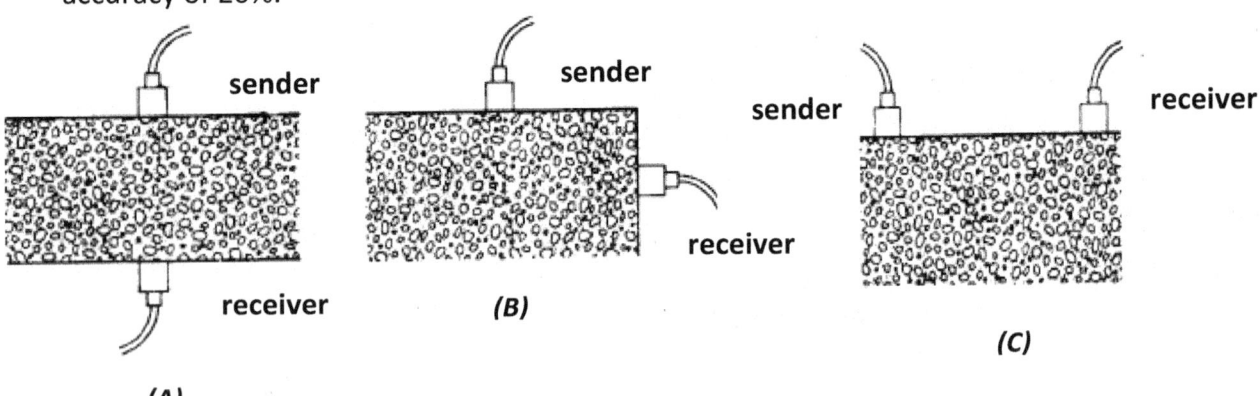

(Figure 3-1) Methods of sending and receiving ultrasonic waves

3-1-1-1 Scope and application

In this method, ie the speed of ultrasonic waves, both the lack of density and the change in the ratio of water to cement are easily determined. However, this method is used to determine the strength of concretes made of different materials with unknown ratios. But it can be used to estimate the strength of concrete in situ.

In fact, due to the fact that higher specific gravity tends to have higher strength, it can be said that there is a general classification based on wave velocity and concrete quality, which are suggested by White hurst [18] for concrete weighing approximately 2400 kg / m3. As shown in the table below.

(Table 3-1) Classification of concrete quality based on wave velocity [18]

Quality of concrete	longitudinal wave velocity (Km / S)
4.5<	Excellent
3.4-5.5	Good
3-3.5	Medium
3-2	Weak
2>	Very weak

The velocity of the waves depends on factors such as the temperature of the concrete at the time of testing, the path length, the size of the aggregates, the type of cement, the moisture, the life or age of the concrete, the presence of reinforcement, the curing conditions, the sample size and the stresses.

3-1-1-2 Scope of application:

1- Estimation of concrete strength quality.
2- Estimating the depth of surface cracks.
3- Determining cracks and layering of concrete cover.

3-1-2 Eschmidt hammer

This test is also known as reflection hammer, impact hammer or hardness test and is a non-destructive method for testing concrete. The experiment is based on the principle that the reflection of a resilient object depends on the hardness of the surface against the object it strikes. Figure (2-3) shows that in the Schmidt hammer there is a mass attached to a spring which is given a constant amount of energy by pulling the spring to a certain point, thus pressing the hammer to the smooth surface of the concrete. After release, the mass is affected by the reflection of the hammer rod (which is still in contact with the concrete surface), and the distance traveled by the mass, expressed as a percentage of the initial expansion of the spring, is called the reflection number. This value is indicated by a symbol that moves along a graduated scale. The number of reflections is an absolute measure, because it depends on the energy stored in the spring and the mass. [19]

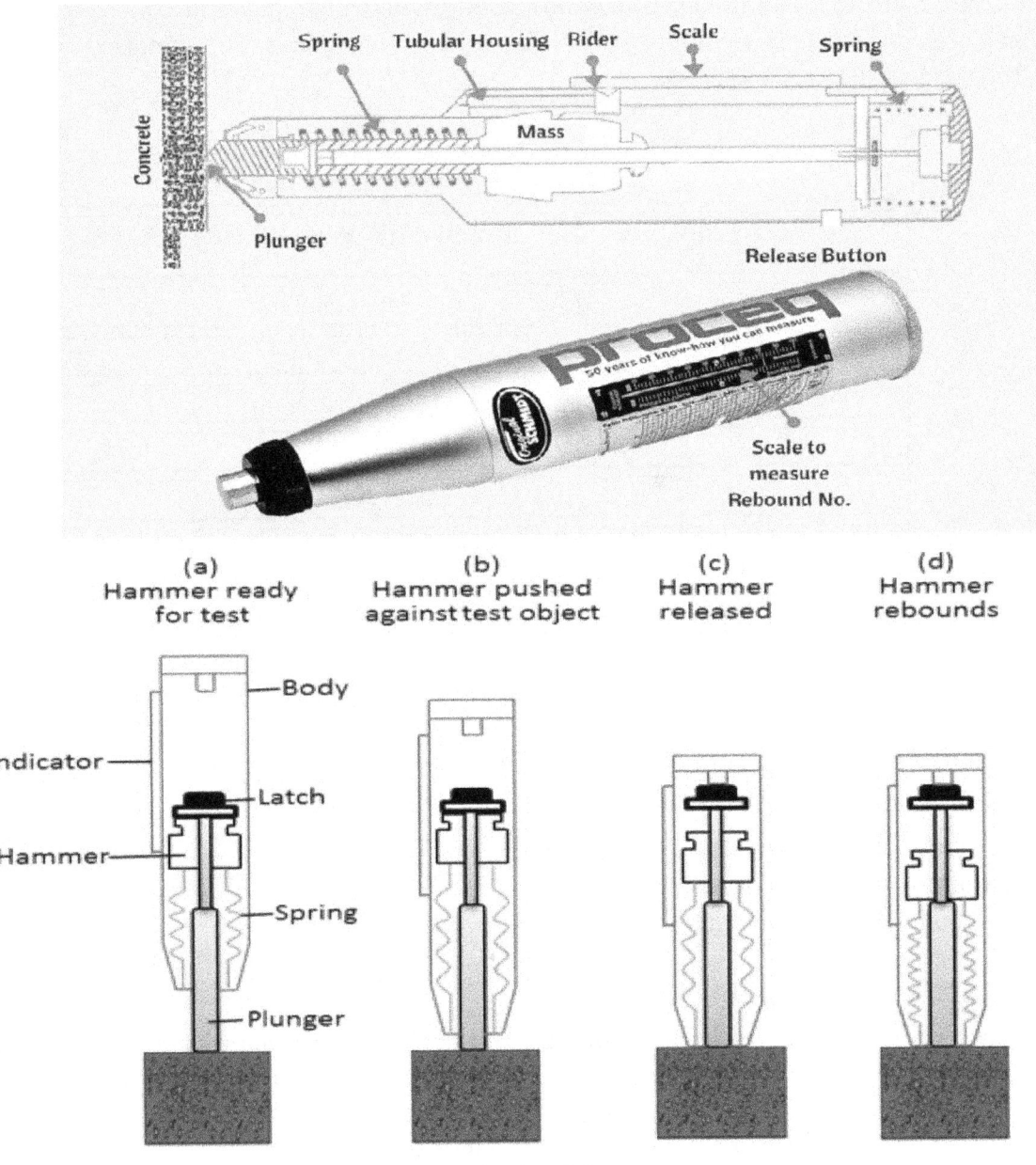

(Figure 3-2) Schmidt hammer

This test is sensitive to the presence of aggregates and bubbles immediately in front of the hammer rod, so it is necessary to perform 10 to 12 readings in the test area. The hammer rod should always be perpendicular to the concrete surface. However, the position of the hammer relative to the vertical affects the reflection number due to the effect of gravity on the motion of the mass. Therefore, for a given concrete, the reflection number is one cup smaller than the reflection number of a roof. [19]

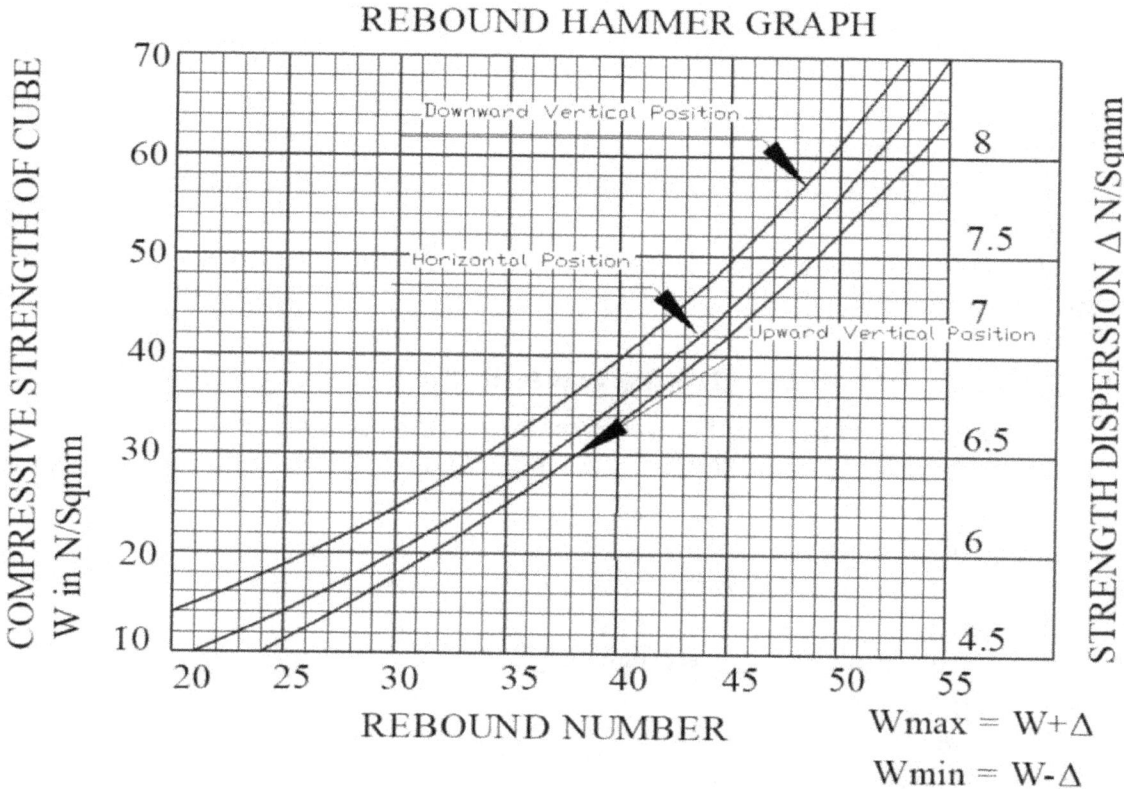

While vertical and inclination levels lead to mediocre results, consideration of such changes is more empirical. There is no equal relationship between hardness and strength of concrete. But for a particular concrete, experimental relationships can be determined. This relationship depends on factors such as the degree of saturation and carbonation, which affect the properties of the concrete surface. As a result, the Schmidt hammer test is useful as a measure of the uniformity and relative quality of concrete in a structure or in the production of a number of precast concrete pieces.

Note:
ASTM C805-79 and BS4408: Part4: 1971 describe this experiment.

3-1-2-1 Scope of application:

1- The application of this method is to express the uniformity of concrete, to determine the weak and poor areas of concrete, as well as the approximate estimation of the in-situ strength of concrete.

2- For a specific mixing design, the number of resistances is affected by factors such as surface moisture, surface polishing methods and depth of carbonation. Carbonation of 50% has an effect on test results.

3- Resilient hammers, even with one name, may be 1 to 3 different in strength, so the test should be done with one hammer.

4- This method is not a basis for rejecting or accepting concrete because it was an approximate method. [20]

3-1-3 The method of penetrating waves in the ground (Crevasse Wave)

The method examines penetrating waves on the ground using electromagnetic energy at frequencies between 50 and 150 MHz below the surface. From this method to detect [21]:

1- Cavities and separation of concrete layer.
2- Location of reinforcements.
3- Determining the thickness of the pavement.
4- Investigation of changes in concrete structure.
5- Specifications of concrete constituent materials such as:
A- The amount of water.
B- degree of hydration.
C. The presence of chloride ions.

Used to detect subsurface characteristics instead of the ground penetration wave method, the short pulse wave method is used for this method.

Using the propagation speed and the amplitude of the recorded electromagnetic waves and their analysis, sub-surface properties or changes in these properties can be obtained. The vertical shape of the electromagnetic wave propagation in one direction is as follows.

$$A_R = A_0(-\alpha x) \, i\omega(t - \frac{x}{v})$$

where in:
A_R = registered domain.
x = distance traveled.

v = phase velocity.
A0 = domain in the state x = 0 and t = 0
α = damping coefficient.
ω = angular frequency.
1=i²

Regardless of the scatter for non-magnetic materials such as concrete and for the high frequencies commonly used to evaluate concrete structures, the phase velocity first depends on the relative dielectric constant of the material.

$$V = \frac{C}{\sqrt{\varepsilon}}$$

C = speed of light in vacuum (m / s 108 × 3)
ε = relative dielectric constant (air equal to one and water approximately 80 and for dry building materials between 4 to 10)
v = phase velocity.

Therefore, the relative dielectric constant of natural and structural materials first changes with the amount of water in the material and in addition it is affected by changes in porosity, mixing ratios, temperature, pore water and the shape of particles and cavities.
In the interface, materials with different electromagnetic properties, some of the waves pass through it and enter the next layer, and the rest of the waves return to the surface and are recorded by the receiver antenna.
The magnitude of the wavelength returning to the surface is a function of the difference between the electromagnetic wavelengths of the two materials, and as this wavelength increases, stronger reflective waves result. For low-frequency materials with high wave frequencies, the reflection coefficient (R) gives the magnitude of the reflected waves as a function of the relative dielectric constants of the higher materials (ε1) and the lower materials (ε2).

$$R = \frac{\sqrt{\varepsilon_1} - \sqrt{\varepsilon_2}}{\sqrt{\varepsilon_1} + \sqrt{\varepsilon_2}}$$

Using this equation and recording the amplitude of the waves, information can be obtained from the existing boundaries, such as the joint of steel and concrete.

The transmitting device consists of a wave generator that transmits the frequency to the transmitting antenna Tx. The reflective waves R that reach the receiver antenna are recorded, but these waves reach the receiver at a certain distance S from the transmitter. Of course, A (in the air) and G (on the ground) waves also reach the receiver and are recorded. (Figure 3-3) and using a wave data display, the boundaries of different layers with different electromagnetic properties are marked in points.

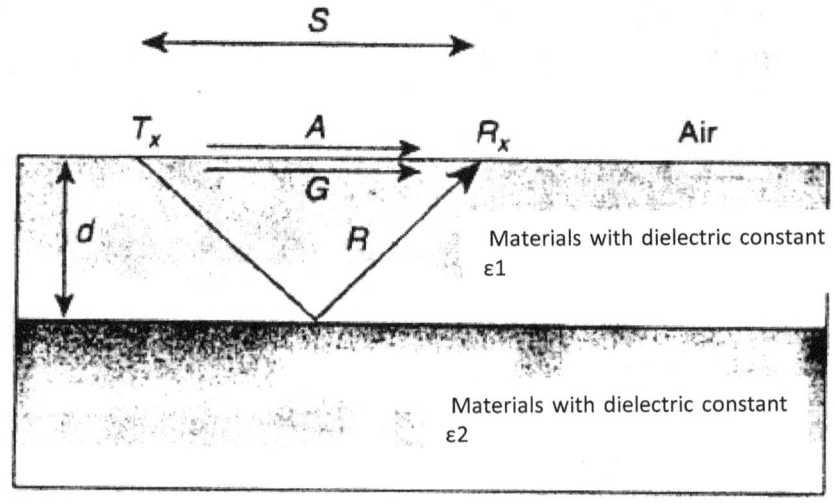

(Figure 3-3) Hold the waves [21]

By removing the ground and air waves and by moving the transmitting antennas, it recorded the location of the reinforcement inside the concrete from its surface [19] and also determined the concrete protrusion that occurs due to the corrosion of the reinforcement. (Figure 3-4)

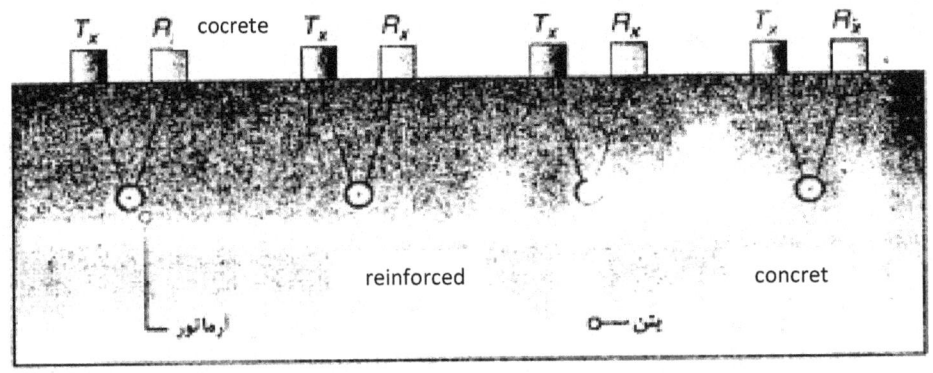

(Figure 3-4) Infiltrate

3-1-4 Reinforced concrete cutting method (Tomography)

A cut-out derived from the Greek word tomos (cut) can be studied by taking images of cross-sections of an object. The application of non-destructive images of the internal structure of an object, including defects, cracks, heterogeneity and heterogeneity is observed.

X-ray cutting method and a suitable method for detecting cracks with a decomposition power of more than 5 micrometers and also determining the location of reinforcement in the structure as usual.

3-1-4-1 Scope of application:

1- Determining the location of reinforcements at a depth of 6 to 7 cm from the concrete surface.
2- Cracks full of water.
3- Corrosion around the armature.

Cutting method is a cheap, fast and easy to use method.

3-2 Semi-destructive experiments

3-2-1 Intrusion resistance test

This test, known commercially as the Windsor rod test. Determines the strength of concrete by the depth of penetration of the metal rod, which is driven into the concrete by applying energy through a special metal gun. The principle of interest in this test is that for standard test conditions, the penetration depth is inversely proportional to the compressive strength of concrete. But the relationship depends on the hardness of the aggregates. Penetration resistance curves are available in terms of aggregate hardness. In practice, however, the penetration resistance must be modified according to the compressive strength of standard test specimens or actual concrete cores used. [19](Figure 3-5)

Similar to the Schmidt hammer test, the penetration resistance test basically measures hardness and does not lead to absolute resistance results.

But the advantage of this test is that it measures the hardness at a certain depth of concrete and not just on its surface. Because the damage caused by the test is resistance to local penetration and it is possible to re-test in the vicinity of the test site. [19]. This test is described in ASTM C803-82.

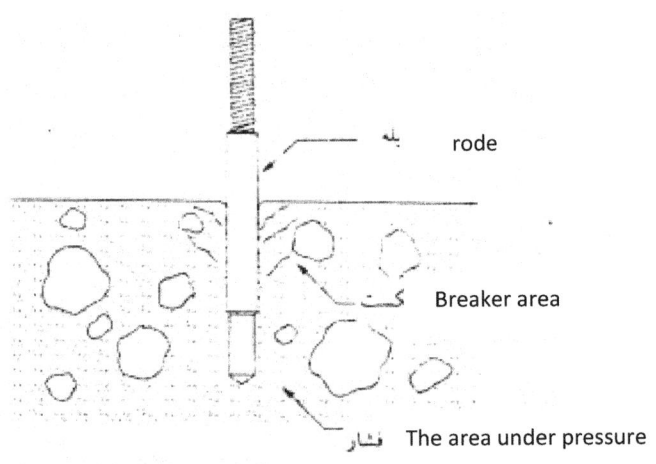

(Figure 3-5) Intrusion resistance

3-2-2-Extraction test (Pullout)

This method, described by ASTM C900-82, measures the force required to pull out a wide-ended steel rod already embedded in concrete. For

The specific shape of the bar, when it is pulled out, a piece of concrete or approximately the same shape is pulled out as an incomplete cone. The pull-out resistance is calculated as the ratio of the force to the ideal surface of the incomplete cone. This resistance is close to the shear strength of concrete. The pulling force in a wide range of storage conditions is related to the compressive strength of standard cores or cylinders. [19](Figure 3-6)

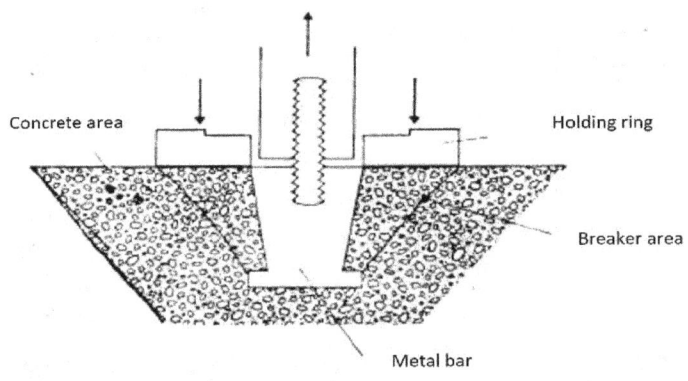

(Figure 3-6) Exhaustion

Extraction tests are usually performed in two ways:
- Installation in mold or lock Test.

- Installation in hardened concrete or capo test.

In the first method, a metal piece is installed in the mold and then concreted. Therefore, testing should be planned before constructing the structure. In the second method, the hardened concrete is drilled and a metal piece is installed inside the core. As a result, this method is more flexible in terms of decision making for testing in each structure. Test points must be at least 200 mm apart. Also, the distance from the center to the edge of the concrete member under test should be at least 100 mm. The metal part must be installed in a position where the reinforcement is outside the rupture cone. Loading system to the brain piece, the load must be applied at a uniform speed. It is recommended to be loading speed $0.5 \pm 0.2 \frac{KN}{S}$ and loading continues until the concrete breaks, but the results are recorded with an accuracy of 0.5 KN. [22]

3-2-2-1 Important points in the extraction method

- In this method, the final load is the same compressive strength that concrete can withstand.

The coefficient of variation of the extraction test is approximately twice that of the cylindrical compression specimen test.

- The size of the aggregates attached to the core has the greatest effect on the difference in the results of the extraction test.

To obtain strength in place of concrete, we need a relationship between compressive strength and tensile strength.

- It is very effective to check the action of concrete to perform the extraction test and determine the test time.

3-2-3 Twist Off method

This new method, which is a semi-destructive test, was invented in 2005 by Dr. Naderi. [23](Figure 3-7)

This method is an accurate method with wide application to determine the strength of concrete in the laboratory and on site as a low-cost semi-destructive test with high working speed and very minor degradation. The difference between this method and other methods is its low cost and partial destruction compared to other methods. The advantages of using this method in any position, horizontal, vertical or sloping surface of the test surface. Another advantage of this test is the simplicity of its method and the lack of previous skills and its availability.

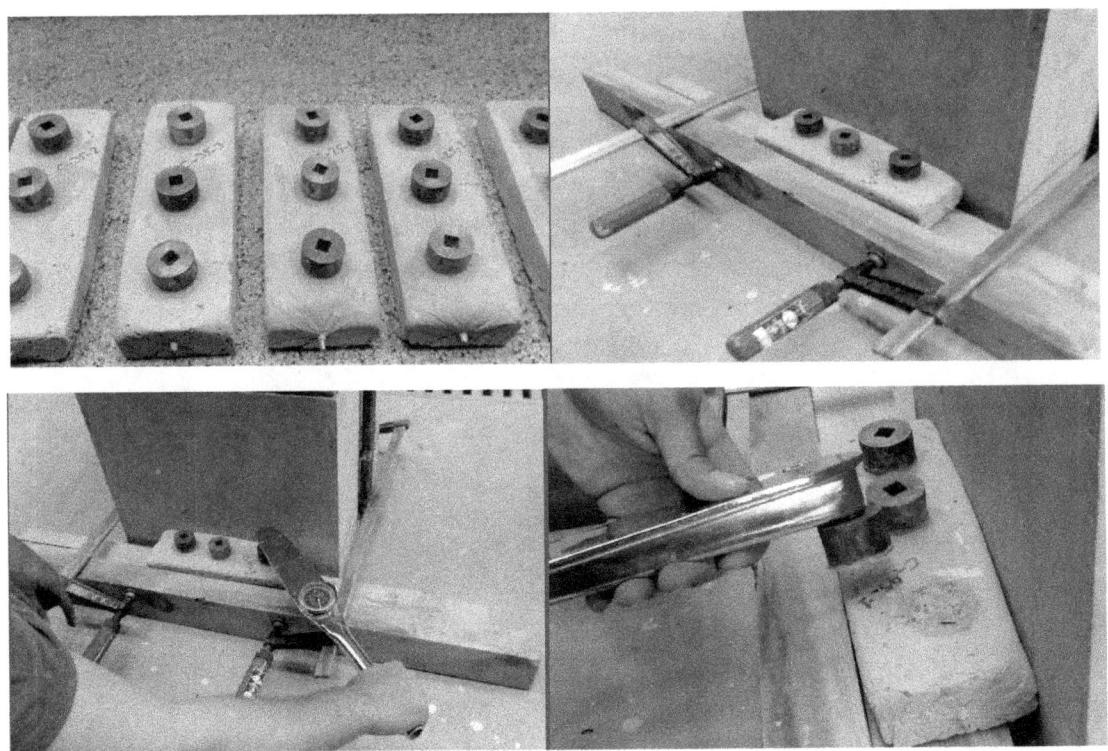

(Figure 3-7) Twist off test method

The test method is that a metal cylinder with a diameter of 40 mm and a height of 25 mm is glued to the place intended for determination of resistance by a two-component epoxy adhesive and then a torsional torque is applied directly to the torque meter. We insert a metal cylinder that this torsional torque is applied continuously and uniformly until the concrete adhering to the cylinder is broken and we record the amount of force by reading the gauge on the crack meter. (Figure 3-7)

(Figure 3-8) As shown in the figure, the failure is very minor.

3-2-3-1 Scope of application

1- Determining the strength of concrete.
2- Determining the process of obtaining concrete strength.
3- Evaluation of existing structures.
4- Determining the time of molding.
5- Determining the shipping time of prefabricated parts.
6- Determining the time of applying the prestressing force.
7- Determining the breakdown process in cases where the failure of the concrete surface is expected to increase over time. [24]

Also, among the advantages of this determination of compressive strength, construction materials such as brick, mortar, plaster and. . . is. In addition, this method is easy to repeat due to the speed of work and low cost and partial destruction.

3-2-4 friction transferring method

One of the semi-destructive methods and tests (invented by Dr. Naderi) is the friction transfer method that was introduced by him in the mid-1980s. [19] This method is an accurate, fast and very practical method for determining the strength of concrete, resin, stones, asphalt and. . . is. One of the most valuable advantages of this method is the determination of strength at different depths of concrete and types of materials. Another advantage is the simplicity of this method. In this method, like the torsion method, it is possible to test all levels of resistance in place of concrete, and also the amount of damage to the tested organ is very small and can be easily repaired. (Figure 3-9)

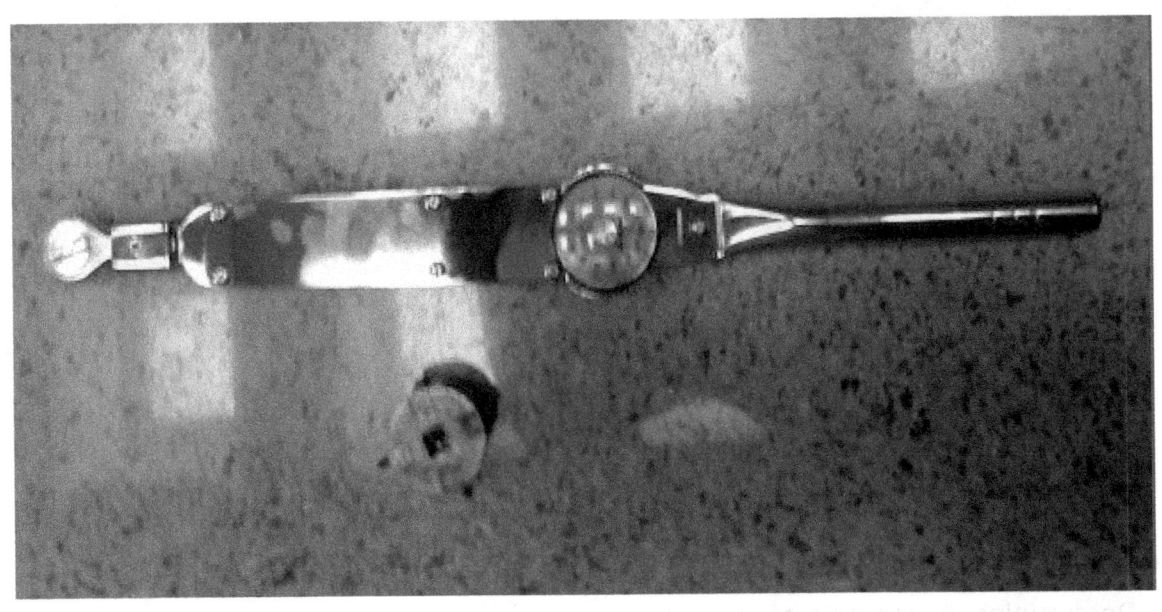

(Figure 3-9) Friction transfer method equipment

(Figure 3-10) Method of performing friction transfer test

In this method, a core with a diameter of 50 mm is created by a coroner device at the test site to a depth of 25 mm. Then we put the transmission device on this core and fasten it with two screws. Now, with a crack meter, we apply torsional torque to the test section and apply this torque continuously and uniformly, until the concrete of the test site is broken, and record the amount of force by reading the gauge on the crack meter. We do. (Figure 3-10)

In this method, the shear strength is related to the compressive strength of concrete and its device is very simple. Many of the factors that cause the results to be scattered have been eliminated and are highly accurate.

3-2-4-1 Scope of application

1- Determining the strength of concrete.
2- General evaluation of structures.
3- Accurate evaluation of places where the guess is in the weakness of the structure in those places.
4- Preventing the scattering of results.
5- Determining the compressive strength of various construction materials.
6- Speed in receiving test results.
7- Determining the strength of concrete at different depths.

Due to the speed and low cost of this method compared to a variety of semi-destructive methods, this method can be used as one of the most accurate and widely used semi-destructive methods.

It should be noted that in order to determine the strength of self-compacting concrete samples that have undergone alkaline silica reaction and ice cycle and ice melting tests. I have used this method in this book and the results of these tests are given in Chapter 5 of this book.

Reference

[1] "The European Guidelines for Self-Compacting Concrete". May 2005

[2] Groth, Patrik. "Fibre Reinforced concrete- fracture mechanics methods applied on self-compacting concrete and energetically modified binders," department of civil engineering division of structural engineering lulea University of technology s-971 87 lulea Sweden, January 2004

[3] Ouchi, Mashiro,"Application of Self-Compacting Concrete in Japan, Europe and the United States", 2003 ISHPC.

[4] Cristian Druta, "Tensile Strength and Bonding Characteristics of Self-Compacting Concrete", the Department of Engineering Science, August 2003, pp. 12, 13

[5] Bouzoubaa,N., Lachemi,M., "Self Compacting Concrete Incorporating

High-Volumes of Class F Fly Ash," International Centre for Sustainable Development of Cement and Concrete (ICON), CANMET/Natural resources Canada

[6] Domone, P.L, "Self-compacting concrete: An analysis of 11 years of case studies". Department of Civil and Environmental Engineering, University College London, London, UK, Received 10 May 2005; accepted11 October 2005,Available online 1 December 2005

[7] Ouchi. Masahiro, "Self-Compacting Concrete development, applications and investigations," Kochi University of Technology, Japan

[8]- Goodier, C.I. 2003. Development of Self-Compacting Concrete.Structures & Building 156, Issue SB4: 405-414,2003

[9] Haykawa, M., Matsuka, Y. and Yokota, K., "Application of Super Workable Concrete in the Construction of 70-Story Building in Japan, "ACI SP-154, Detroit, 1995.

[10] www.southtravels.com/europe/switzerland/crowneplazageneva

[11] "EFNARC Specification and Guidelines for Self- Compacting Concrete," Feb. 2002.

[12] G. De Schatter, "Guidelines for Testing Fresh Self-Compacting Concrete," September 2005. p.4

[13] Victor C. Li, H.J. Kong, Yin-Wen Chan, "Development of Self-Compacting Engineered Cementitious Composites" p.4

[14] European Union Growth Contract No. G6RD-CT-2001-00580, "Measurement of properties of fresh self-compacting concrete," Final Report: September 2005. p.2

[15] Sonebi, Mohammed. "Medium strength self-compacting concrete containing fly ash: Modeling using factorial experimental plans," Advanced Concrete and Masonry Centre, University of Paisley, Paisley PA1 2BE, Scotland, UK,Received 21 April 2003; accepted 8 December 2003

[16] Peter JM Bartos, "Testing SCC", Measurement of properties of fresh Self-compacting concrete, ACM Centre, University of Paisley, Scotland, UK & E-CORE Network, p 12

[17] Guide Book on Non Destructive Testing of Concrete Structures, Training Course Series, No.17, International Atomic Energy Agency, Vienna, 2002, p.p.1-78 and 100-129.

[18] Hand Book on Repair and Rehabilitation of RCC Buildings CPWD, Mayapuri, New Delhi, First Published in 2002, Chapter 3, p.p.13-28.

[19] Neville and Brussels, "Concrete Technology", translated by Ramezanipour, A. And Shah Nazari, m. Twelfth edition, Azarang Publications, Tehran, 2005

[20] Malhotra, V.M. Testing Hardened Concrete Nondestructive Methods, ACI Monograph No.9, American Concrete Institute, 2003. Chapter 1-8.

[21] Mahta and Monteiro "Methods of non-destructive evaluation of concrete" Translated by Ali Akbar Ramezanianpour First edition of Amirkabir University of Technology Publications in 2006.

[22] British Standard 1881, Method for Determination of the compressive Strength of Concrete Cores, Part 120, British Standards Institution, London, 1983.

[23] Naderi, Mahmoud - Patent in the Companies Registration and Industrial Property Office, Pishsh method, 2005.

[24] Madani, Saeed - Twisting method for measuring concrete strength - Master Thesis, Imam Khomeini International University, Qazvin, 2006.

www.ingramcontent.com/pod-product-compliance
Lightning Source LLC
Chambersburg PA
CBHW081637040426
42449CB00014B/3353